Se

Pota

Katy Scott

THANKS FOR YOUR SUPPORT

From drawing book supremo Katy Scott this is a book where you can
add your funny, magical or simply just wrong remarks.
It's unauthorized and is intended to be satirical.
It's a charming book that is interactive and allows you to be playful and
creative with your own artwork.

Drawing books aren't just for kids any more.
You know that life can sometimes be a a little busier and more
complicated.

With this book, it almost has magical powers:
You receive it, you write in it and it will make you laugh. (only if you've
written something funny.)

If you write something particularly funny and share it, it could become
viral, you could become famous, and you could become rich.
What other book could promise so much?

As you can appreciate: It's an unofficial satirical book.

There are some other titles in the series.

Feel free to contact me on Twitter
with your funny examples,
feedback or suggestions.
@KindleKatyScott

Well done! You have bought or been bought the award winning book, Sexy Potatoes. Probably because you know they are the sexiest vegetable of all time. The way they give you the eye and hubba bubba they're just wow!

There are also some potatoes that you can dress up, draw on, or simply admire. Have fun!

This is me. Do you think I'm sexy?

Look at these potatoes.

A family of foxy potatoes.

An orgy of potatoes, the police are trying to get to the root of the problem.

A smiler

Oh la la la

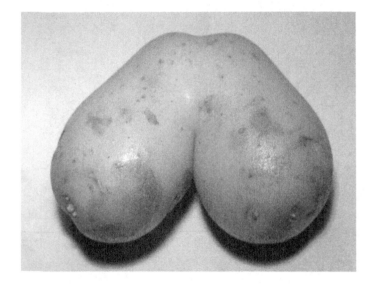

Taylor Swift

Kylie Jenner

Kanye West

Ed Sheeran

Seductive Potatoes

Heart Potato

An alluring bunch of potatoes

A shapely potato with a coarse side.

A racy lot of potatoes

My heart shaped potato

A get-together

We come in all shapes and sizes

Sensual and sensuous.

A provoking lot of potatoes

Fanciable Potatoes

X rated potato

Hot and foxy potatoes

An erotic collection of potatoes

Sizzling Potatoes

A slinky and tempting potato, the one in the middle.

They all have come to bed eyes.

Romance

Too many to choose from

Erotic potatoes

Your Potato

Your Potato

Your Potato

Your Potato

Your Potato

Your Potato

Your Potato

Your Potato

Your Potato

Your Potato

Your Potato

Your Potato

Your Potato

Your Potato

Your Potato

Your Potato

Your Potato

Your Potato

Your Potato

Your Potato

Your Potato

Your Potato

Your Potato

Your Potato

Your Potato

Your Potato

Your Potato

Your Potato

Your Potato

Your Potato

Your Potato

Your Potato

Your Potato

Your Potato

Your Potato

Your Potato

Your Potato

Your Potato

Your Potato

Your Potato

Your Potato

Your Potato

Your Potato

Your Potato

Your Potato

Your Potato

Your Potato

Your Potato

Your Potato

Your Potato

Your Potato

Your Potato

Your Potato

Your Potato

Your Potato

Your Potato

Your Potato

Your Potato

Your Potato

Your Potato

Your Potato

Your Potato

Your Potato

Your Potato

Your Potato

Printed in Great Britain
by Amazon